What Islam Says about Domestic Violence

A Guide for Helping Muslim Families

What Islam Says About Domestic Violence

A Guide for Helping Muslim Families

Zainab Alwani, MS
&
Salma Abugideiri, MEd, LPC

© Copyright 1424AH/2003AC

FAITH
FOUNDATION FOR APPROPRIATE AND
IMMEDIATE TEMPORARY HELP

All rights reserved.
No part of this book may be reproduced or transmitted in any form or by any means electronic or mechanical, including photocopy, or recording, or any information storage and retrieval system, without permission in writing from the publisher.

Copies of
WHAT ISLAM SAYS ABOUT DOMESTIC VIOLENCE
– A GUIDE FOR HELPING MUSLIM FAMILIES
are available from the publisher:
FOUNDATION FOR APPROPRIATE AND IMMEDIATE TEMPORARY HELP
500 Grove Street, Suite 210, Herndon, VA 20172
Phone: (571) 323-2198
E-mail: info@faithus.org
Website: www.faithus.org

TABLE OF CONTENTS

Acknowledgments 7

Introduction 9

Overview of Islamic Paradigm 12

Core Values 14

Dealing with oppression 16

Concept of Marriage 18

Family Structure 19

Gender Roles 20

Decision-Making in the Family 21

Parent-Child Relationship 24

Domestic Violence 26

Resolving Conflict 28

Divorce: A Peaceful Solution 33

Child Custody 36

Tools for the Worker 37
      Power & Control Wheel: Islamic Perspective 37
      Concept of Accountability 44
      Useful Interventions with Muslims.................... 46

Appendix 1: Compilation of verses used in this paper 53

Appendix 2: Power & Control Wheel 61

Additional Readings & Useful Websites 62

Acknowledgments

The writing of this guide was made possible by the collaborative efforts of FAITH (Foundation for Appropriate and Immediate Temporary Help, Herndon, VA), CMHS (Center for Multicultural Human Services, Falls Church, VA), and IIIT (International Institute of Islamic Thought). It was funded in part by the Department of Criminal Justice V-Stop grant to CMHS, FAITH and by IIIT. The project was initiated and coordinated by Ambreen Ahmed, Director of the Safe and Peaceful Families program at FAITH.

The authors wish to acknowledge the feedback and suggestions of Dr Jamal Barzinji, Imam Mohamed Magid, Dr. Taha Jabir Alalwani, Imam Johari Abdul-Malik, Dr. Mohamad A. El Sheikh, Imam Faizul R. Khan, and Imam Nahiddian.

Introduction

This guide is written for anyone working in the area of domestic violence: advocates, police officers, mental health workers, shelter staff, medical providers, lawyers, etc. It is intended to be used as a training supplement for those who work in this field, with specific reference to the Power and Control Wheel.[1] It was written as a result of many questions and concerns presented by workers who deal with Muslim women and families. Because the religion of Islam and the culture of the Middle East are relatively unfamiliar to most workers in this country, dealing with the Muslim population is often challenging and confusing.

This guide is an attempt to explain the perspective of the religion of Islam on the issue of domestic violence. Islam is a religion followed by approximately 7 million people in the United States.[2] These Muslims come from different ethnic and educational backgrounds. One-third of the Muslims in the U.S. come from South Asian (India, Pakistan, Bangladesh, and Afghanistan). Thirty percent of Muslims in the US are African-American, and twenty-five percent are Arab.[2] There are many myths and misunderstandings surrounding the religion of Islam. It is important to note that while the Arab culture is often associated with the teachings of Islam, only one-fifth of the world's Muslims are Arab. Some

---

1. Developed in 1984 in the Women's Support Group & Batter's Group; Domestic Abuse Intervention Project, 202 East Superior Street, Duluth, Minnesota 55802, 218-722-2781
www.duluth-model.org. See Appendix 2 for copy.
2. www.cair-net.org/asp/aboutislam.asp

of the countries with the largest Muslim populations are Indonesia, India and China. Ethnic background, culture, and level of education are some of the variables that affect the ways Islam is practiced and applied, leading to significant diversity among Muslims at least at a surface level. However, the basic teachings and tenets of Islam are the same for all Muslims, regardless of their roots or heritage.

It is beyond the scope of this guide to give a complete overview of the religion or to talk about the impact of culture on religious practice and understanding. The goal of this guide is to present an overview of the teachings of Islam as related to the subject of domestic violence. It is hoped that having this understanding will guide workers to more effective and more sensitive interventions with Muslim victims of domestic violence.

Readers will note that the primary sources used in this guide to define the Islamic perspective on domestic violence are the Holy Qur'an and the traditions of the Prophet Muhammad (PBUH).[4] The Holy Qur'an is accepted by all Muslims as the direct word of God[5] revealed to His last messenger, Muhammad (PBUH).[6] The Qur'an is regarded as a primary source of guidance for all Muslims, and its teachings were exemplified by the life of Muhammad (PBUH) as a model for all mankind to follow. His behavior and sayings are collected in the

---

4. Abbreviation for peace be upon him.

5. The Arabic word for God is "*Allah*".

6. Muslims accept and believe in all of the prophets beginning with Adam and including Abraham, Moses and Jesus (peace be on them all). Muhammad is the last prophet, who brought the revelation of Islam to the Arabian peninsula. Islam is viewed as the continuation of the same message brought by previous prophets. Muslims follow Prophet Muhammad as a model for their behavior and way of life.

Traditions[7] or Sunnah and are referred to for practical implementation of Qur'anic guidelines, principles and teachings.

The Qur'an was revealed in Arabic, and this Arabic text has been preserved in its original form from the time of its revelation over 1400 years ago until today. While the Qur'an has been translated in most of the world's languages, only the original text is accepted as divine. Translations or interpretations of the Qur'an may differ from each other, depending on the translator's historical, educational and cultural context. Many different translations exist. Some translations or interpretations may lead to different and sometimes incorrect conclusions about the meanings of a particular verse. Although an authentic English translation is provided in this paper[8], it is important to note that both authors referenced the original Arabic text for the research and conclusions presented here.

---

7. The collections of Traditions, or *Hadith*, used for this paper are by Bukhari, Muslim, & Tirmidhi.

8. Ali, Abdullah Yusuf. (1989). *The Meaning of Holy Qur'an.* New Edition. Brentsville, MD: Amana Publications.

Overview of The Islamic Paradigm

Islam teaches that human beings are created by God to worship Him, and that they are directly accountable to God for their behavior. The Qur'an teaches that God has given people the freedom to choose which path to take in every decision of life. He has also outlined the consequences of these choices.[9] On the Day of Judgment, every person will be held accountable for choices made during his/her life and will either be rewarded with eternal Paradise or punished in Hell. This concept of accountability is central to the Islamic paradigm in general, and has particular relevance to the prevention and treatment of domestic violence. It will be addressed in detail later in this guide.

In Islam, no human being has the right to control another human being's life. Even the Prophet Muhammad (PBUH) was reminded by God that he could not force people to believe in his message of monotheism. He did not have the authority to control others, but only to advise, remind and guide them.[10] Even in matters of religion, the most important aspect of our lives, individuals are given free will. The Qur'an says, *"Let there be no compulsion in religion. Truth stands out clear from error. Whoever rejects evil and believes in God has grasped the most trustworthy Handhold, that never breaks"* (2:256).

---

9. *"Say, the truth is from your Lord. Let him who will, believe, and let him who will, reject (it): For the wrongdoers We have prepared a fire whose smoke and flames, like the walls and roof of a tent, will hem them in....As to those who believe and work righteousness...for them will be gardens of Eternity, beneath them rivers will flow..."* (18:29-31)

10. *"Therefore do give admonition, for you are one to admonish. You are not one to manage (people's) affairs. But if any turns away and rejects God, God will punish him with a mighty punishment."* (88:21-24).

Islam presents a comprehensive model for all aspects of life. Many of the guidelines and principles taught by Islam form a framework designed to prevent individual and social problems at all levels of society. Because the family is considered to be the basic unit of society, family relationships are specifically protected by rules that guard against potential abuse. While many other aspects of life are guided by broad principles and values, teachings related to the protection of a healthy family unit are given with great detail in the Qur'an and in the teachings of the Prophet Muhammad (PBUH).

Core Values [11]

In order to conceptualize the Islamic paradigm and to have an appreciation for the preventive proactive model that is prescribed by Islamic teachings, it is important to understand the core Islamic values of Justice, Equality, and Freedom. These values are inter-related, and one cannot exist without the other. Actions that violate any of these values is not acceptable in Islam.

Justice

Justice is the overriding value: *"God commands justice, the doing of good, and liberality to kith and kin, and He forbids all shameful deeds, and injustice and rebellion. He instructs you, that you may receive admonition"*(16:90). The Qur'an also says, *"O you who believe! Stand out firmly for God as witnesses to fair dealing, and let not the hatred of others to you make you swerve to wrong and depart you from justice. Be just: that is next to piety. And fear God. For God is well-acquainted with all that you do"* (5:8). Regarding matters at the domestic level, the Qur'an says, *"O you who believe! Stand out firmly for justice, as witnesses to God, even as against yourselves, or your parents, or your kin, and whether it be (against) rich or poor: for God can protect you both. Follow not the lusts (of your hearts), lest you swerve and if you distort (justice) or decline to do justice, verily God is well-acquainted with all that you do"* (4:135).

---

11. Adapted from Rabi`, Hamid. *Nazariyat al Qiyam as-Siyasiyyah*. Cairo, Egypt, 1972.

Equality

Islam teaches that all people are created equal in worth and value regardless of race, ethnicity, gender or class. The concept of equality is expressed in, *"O mankind! Reverence your guardian-Lord, who created you from a single soul. Created, of like nature, its mate, and from them twain scattered (like seeds) countless men and women—fear God, through Whom you demand your mutual (rights), and (reverence) the wombs (that bore you*[12]*), for God ever watches over you"*(4:1). The only aspect by which one person is deemed better than another in the sight of God is that of piety. *"O mankind! We created you from a single (pair) of a male and a female, and made you into nations and tribes, that you may know each other (not that you may despise each other). Verily, the most honored of you in the sight of God is the most righteous of you..."* (49:13).

Freedom

The third value is freedom. It includes freedom of thought, freedom of speech, and freedom of religion. Freedom is not unlimited or absolute; it is the freedom that God has given humanity to choose between right and wrong. It is a freedom that is balanced by responsibility towards God and the belief that ultimately, every person will be held accountable for his/her actions.

---

12. Refers to women, in general, and specifically mothers.

Dealing with Oppression

Behavior which violates justice, equality and freedom leads to oppression, which is strictly forbidden. Of course, oppression occurs in all populations including Muslim families, and it exists in many forms. Victims of oppression are encouraged to view their experiences as a test from God. They are expected to strive to find solutions, while exercising patience and forgiveness. *"The blame is only against those who oppress people with wrongdoing and insolently transgress beyond bounds through the land, defying right and justice. For such (people) there will be a grievous penalty. But indeed if any show patience and forgive, that would truly be an exercise of courageous will and resolution in the conduct of affairs"* (Q 42:42-43). This does not mean that victims should be passive. On the contrary, Muslims are instructed by the Qur'an to be strong and to seek justice. *"And those who, when an oppressive wrong is inflicted on them, (are not cowed) but help and defend themselves. The recompense for an injury is an injury equal thereto (in degree), but if a person forgives and makes reconciliation, his reward is due from God, for (God) loves not those who do wrong"* (Q 42: 39-40).[13]

Sometimes experiencing oppression within the family may lead the victim to make choices in violation of Islamic teachings. For example,

---

13. Also, *"We ordained therein for them: life for life, eye for eye, nose for nose, ear for ear, tooth for tooth, and wounds equal for equal. But if anyone remits the retaliation by way of charity, it is an act of atonement for himself. And if any fail to judge by (the light of) what God has revealed, they are (no better than) wrongdoers."* (5:45)

when anger and resentment build due to continuous mistreatment, a victim may find herself wanting to hurt the batterer verbally or physically. In extreme cases, the victim may even kill the batterer. While the anger and resentment are justified, options that are protective and preventive of further harm to either party should be explored. In these situations it is better to leave the abusive situation than to commit any wrongdoing. The Qur'an says, *"When angels take the souls of those who die in sin against their souls, they say, "In what (plight) were you?" They reply, "Weak and oppressed were we in the earth." They say, "Was not the earth of God spacious enough for you to move yourselves away (from evil)?" Such [people] will find their abode in hell—what an evil refuge! Except those who are (really) weak and oppressed—men, women, and children who have no means in their power, nor (a guide-post) to direct their way. For those there is hope that God will forgive. For God does blot out (sins) and is oft- forgiving"* (4:98-99).

Implementing consequences for oppressive or unjust behavior is the responsibility of the society through its established authorities. Individuals do not have the authority to carry out punishments as vigilantes; rather, recourse should follow established channels and procedures with punishment determined and enforced by the legal system.

The Concept of Marriage

The foundation of an Islamic marriage is described in the following verse from the Holy Qur'an: *"And among His signs is this: that He created for you mates from among yourselves, that you may dwell in tranquility with them, and He has put love and mercy between your (hearts). Verily in that are signs for those who reflect"* (30:21). This verse can be taken as a reminder that spouses are inherently equal, and that the union between them is a peaceful and compassionate one. Marriage is considered in Islam to be an act of obedience to God, and the goal of each person within the marriage is to please God by living a divinely guided life and avoiding His prohibitions. Any behavior or interaction done with the intent of upholding divine instruction will be rewarded by God in the hereafter and will contribute to a healthy family unit.

Likewise, all behaviors that violate divine instruction, including the foundation of mercy and love, are punishable by God. Islam prohibits any form of oppression, which could be defined as "an unjust or cruel exercise of authority or power."[14] A legal premise used by Muslim jurists to interpret and judge according to Islamic law can be translated as "Do not do harm, nor allow any harm to be done to you." Oppression occurs when mercy and justice are ignored. Islam defines oppression as transgressing limits or boundaries defined by God, and it prohibits oppression at all levels of society.

---

14. Webster's *Ninth New Collegiate Dictionary*, 1983.

Family Structure

Islam defines the family, not the individual, as the basic unit of society. Within the family, each individual's primary role is to worship and obey God. Thus, God is the ultimate authority to whom each member is accountable. The Qur'an outlines a general structure for the family, but each Muslim family will have its unique characteristics and qualities, as well as specific manners in which members interact with each other. These differences are a result of various cultures, educational background, socio-economic status, etc.

It is not uncommon for Muslim families to live in extended family situations. Adult children are expected to care for their aging parents. In some cultures, there is the "family home" which belongs to the parents but may also be home to married children and their offspring. The extended family provides support on multiple levels, including financial and emotional. Even if nuclear families live separately from the extended family, there are strong emotional ties. During times of crisis, or when major decisions need to be made, the whole family often becomes involved. In many countries, including the United States, if there is conflict between spouses, the wife may stay with her family until the situation is diffused. Extended family members may be turned to for intervention when the couple is unable to resolve a problem on their own

GENDER ROLES

The Qur'an establishes the man as the head of the household, responsible for maintaining the family financially.[15] He is responsible for providing for a broad range of needs, including spiritual, emotional, and educational needs. Without this divine injunction, some men may not fulfill their financial responsibility towards their family. Women are then free to take care of the family by providing nurturing, especially to children. Men and women are partners in the endeavor of having a healthy family unit in which children are raised to be God-conscious members of society. While men are obligated to work in order to provide for the family, women are under no obligation to do so and may or may not choose to work outside the home, depending on the individual circumstances of the family.

The fact that husband and wife have different roles to play in the family does not in any way suggest that men are better than, or have God-given power over, women. The Qur'an sets up the framework for different roles that are equal in value and are complementary. Each gender has special qualities that, in general, lead each gender to be better qualified for a particular role. The Qur'an says, *"And in nowise covet those things in which God has bestowed His gifts more freely on some of you than on others: to men is allotted what they earn, and to women what they earn. But ask God of His bounty. For God has full knowledge of all things."* (4:32).

---

15. *"Men are the protectors and maintainers of women, because God has given the one more than the other, and because of the sustenance they provide from their own means..."* (4:34).

Furthermore, the roles are not mutually exclusive. Both parents must be involved in raising the children. Although each may participate in different aspects of the child's upbringing, they are equally responsible for the overall welfare of the child. The fact that women are the primary managers of household affairs does not mean that husbands should not help, or that they are restricted exclusively to this role. Prophet Muhammad (PBUH), the model husband, used to help with domestic chores such as sweeping and mending his clothes[16]; and his wife Aisha became noted as a leader and a teacher whom many men consulted after the Prophet's death.

---

16. Abu Shaqqah, *Tahrir al-Mar'ah,* V. 1, pp. 128-129.

DECISION-MAKING IN THE FAMILY

In all matters pertaining to the family, husband and wife should consult one another and try to come to a mutually agreeable decision. Mutual consultation is the standard to be used by anyone in a leadership position, as exemplified by the Prophet Muhammad (PBUH). He often consulted his followers and his wives in any matter in which he did not receive divine instruction. In verses that describe the qualities of the believers in general, the Qur'an says, "...those who avoid the greater crimes and shameful deeds, and, when they are angry even then forgive; those who hearken to their Lord, and establish regular prayer; *who (conduct) their affairs by mutual consultation*..."(2:37-38). Because the purpose of any leadership role in Islam is not control and power, but rather, to safeguard the best interest of the group, there is no fear of losing authority on the part of the leader by consulting with the members of that group.

As far as the family is concerned, mutual consultation is specifically mentioned in the matter of weaning the child of divorced parents in two different verses.[17] It is interesting to note that breastfeeding is generally considered to be an issue in the "woman's domain," however, the father

---

17. *"Let the women live in the same style as you live, according to your means: Do not annoy them, so as to restrict them, and if they carry (life in their wombs) spend your substance on them until they deliver their burden, and if they suckle your children give them their recompense: and take mutual counsel together according to what is just and reasonable, and if you find yourselves in difficulties, let another woman suckle the child on the father's behalf."* (65:6)

is included in the decision-making process.[18] Likewise, many areas that are typically considered to be "men's business" should include the opinion of the women, especially when the decisions taken affect the whole family.

---

18. *"The mothers shall give suck to their offspring for two whole years, if the father desires to complete the term. But he shall bear the cost of their food and clothing on equitable terms. No soul shall have a burden laid on it greater than it can bear. No mother shall be treated unfairly on account of her child. Nor father on account of his child, an heir shall be chargeable in the same way. If they both decide on weaning by mutual consent, and after due consultation, there is no blame on them. If you decide on a wet-nurse for your offspring there is no blame on you provided you pay (the mother) what you offered, on equitable terms. But fear God and know that God sees well what you do."* 2:233 (It was a common practice in Arabia for a wet-nurse to be hired to breastfeed the child)

PARENT-CHILD RELATIONSHIP

Islam structures the parent-child relationship very clearly. Islam assigns complete responsibility for raising children to the parents. Their duties include, besides physical care and nourishment, acculturation into Islam and socialization into the Muslim community. The Qur'an explains in detail[19] the rights and obligations for both sides of the relationship under different circumstances. Parents are asked to take good care of their children and to do their duty before asking for their rights. The following example, in the Qur'an, of a righteous man instructing his son highlights the priorities of a Muslim parent: *"O my son! Join not in worship (others) with God: for false worship is indeed the highest wrongdoing...If there be (but) the weight of a mustard seed and it were (hidden) in a rock, or anywhere in the heavens or on the earth, God will bring it forth: For God understands the finer mysteries and is well- acquainted (with them). O my son! Establish regular prayer, enjoin what is just, and forbid what is wrong, and bear with patient constancy whatever betide thee; for this is firmness (of purpose) in the conduct of affairs. And swell not thy cheek with pride at men, nor walk in insolence through the earth; for God loves not any arrogant boaster. And be moderate in pace, and lower thy voice; for the harshest of sounds without doubt is the braying of the donkey."*(31:12-19)

Knowledge is a necessary qualification for the implementation of raising children, but it is not sufficient. God advises the Prophet Muhammad (PBUH) to *"Invite to the way of your Lord with wisdom and*

---

19. Holy Qur'an: 31:12-19, 17:23-25, 46:17-19, 29:8...

beautiful preaching; and argue with them in ways that are best and most gracious."(16:125). In addition to knowledge, wisdom and proper communication etiquette are required to facilitate giving good advice. Even in instances when there is direct violation of God's commands, one may not be harsh. As the Prophet was told, *"It is part of the mercy of God that thou dost deal gently with them. Wert thou severe or harsh-hearted, they would have broken away from about thee: so pass over (their faults), and ask for (God's) forgiveness for them; and consult them in affairs (of moment)*(3:159)

Unfortunately, in some contemporary Muslim families, one sees in many cases, boys are given more liberties than girls to go out, to drive, to pursue higher degrees, and even to participate in Islamic activities. On a more subtle level, Middle Eastern culture gives women the burden of making relationships work out by teaching them to be passive and submissive, sacrificing their needs for their husbands' desires. Although many Muslim families may exhibit these traits, it is important to distinguish between what a family may practice because of their cultural background versus what the religion of Islam actually teaches. It is also important to remember that Muslims, like members of any other faith group, vary in the degree to which they practice their religion or understand its concepts.

Domestic Violence

Although the specific term "Domestic Violence" has not been used traditionally in Muslim cultures, and while there has been some denial historically that domestic violence is a phenomenon that exists in Muslim communities, the Qur'an identifies the concept of domestic violence under the umbrella of oppression. At the family level, oppression is defined as any act that violates the specific boundaries delineated by God[20] to protect spousal and children's rights. The general categories of domestic oppression mentioned in the Qur'an include aggression, wrongdoing, harsh treatment (especially preventing a woman from the choice of marrying whom she pleases), and inflicting harm or injury.[21] Actions that fall into any of these categories are in violation of the Islamic values of justice, equality, freedom, mercy and forgiveness.

Family structure, gender roles, marriage and divorce laws, reconciliation and financial matters are among the issues that are addressed in great detail in the Qur'an. Throughout the many verses discussing these issues, there are common themes which emphasize the connection between justice and piety, accountability to God, and the importance of preventive measures to avoid injustice and oppression.

---

20. See 2: 227-237.
21. The Arabic terms used in the Qur'an for these categories are: *'udwaan, 'adhl,* and *darar.*

Men (husbands, fathers, brothers, or guardians) are warned not to use their authority as head of the household to hurt or take advantage of women in any way. They are reminded that if they do so, they will be ultimately hurting themselves since they will be held accountable by God, with a serious punishment for oppressors. In times of conflict or discord, the reminder of being God-conscious in making choices and decisions is repeated over and over.[22] These reminders emphasize the relationship between each individual and God as over-riding the spousal relationship, or any other human relationship.

---

22. See Qur'an 65:1-12 for details concerning separation, divorce, reconciliation, punishment for transgressors and reward for those who obey God's laws.

Resolving Conflict

Even the best relationships go through difficult times, and the Qur'an provides a formula for dealing with marital discord. The greatest threat to the survival of a marriage comes from infidelity. The steps that are outlined in the following verses serve to deal with this problem and to prevent problems from escalating. *"Men shall take full care of women with the bounties which God has bestowed more abundantly on the former than on the latter, and with what they may spend out of their possessions. And the righteous women are the truly devout ones, who guard the intimacy which God has [ordained to be guarded]. And as for those women whose ill-will you have reason to fear, admonish them [first]; then leave them alone in bed; then beat them; and if thereupon they pay you heed*[23]*, do not seek to harm them. Behold, God is indeed most high, great! And if you have reason to fear that a breach might occur between a [married] couple, appoint an arbiter from among his people and an arbiter from among her people; if they both want to set things aright, God may bring about their reconciliation. Behold, God is indeed all-knowing, aware."*[24] (4:34-35).

Aspects of this verse have been subject to a great deal of controversy among Muslims, as well as different interpretations by Muslim scholars depending on the historical and cultural context in which they

---

23. Yusuf Ali's translation is "if they return to obedience." It should be noted that obedience here is in the context of obedience to God. The husband, as head of the family, is responsible for encouraging his family to be obedient to God, as he himself must be obedient to God.

24. 4:34-35. Translation from Asad, *Muhammad. The Message of the Qur'an*, 1980.

lived. In this verse, the word translated as "ill-will" has been explained by the translator Muhammad Asad as a "deliberate, persistent breach of her marital obligations."[25] He notes that the Prophet Muhammad (pbuh) is not known to have ever hit any woman, and that he "stipulated that beating should be resorted to only if the wife has become guilty, in an obvious manner, of immoral conduct, and that it should be done in such a way as not to cause pain."[26] Muslim scholars agree that if the intention of this verse refers to literally hitting one's wife, it is a symbolic hitting, using nothing harder than the equivalent of a paper tissue. There is consensus that leaving any marks or injury to any degree is unacceptable. A contemporary researcher analyzed this verse within the overall framework of the Qur'an and concluded that in this context, the intended meaning is not "beat", but rather the temporary separation of a husband from his wife.[27]

This verse has often been used by men to justify beating their wives. However, it is important to read this verse in the context provided by the Qur'an in its entirety, as well as by the example of the Prophet Muhammad. A leading contemporary Muslim jurist, Dr. Taha Jabir Al-alwani[28], explained that jurists consider the purposes of marriage when deriving rulings from these verses. The general purposes of marriage include fulfilling the conditions needed for living in tranquility and harmony, building family relationships and networks, and procreation.

---

25. Asad, p. 109, footnote # 44.

26. Asad, p. 110, footnote # 45, views of various scholars are compared.

27. For the complete analysis and discussion, see Abusulayman, Abdulhamid A.(2003). *Marital Discord: Recapturing the Full Islamic Spirit of Human Dignity*. London: The International Institute of Islamic Thought.

28. Personal Communication, Taha Jabir Al-alwani, President of the Graduate School of Islamic Social Sciences, Leesburg, Virginia.

Application of teachings from the Qur'an must not undermine these goals. Sometimes, jurists apply the literal meaning of a verse when that meaning will achieve these goals; other times they apply the spirit of a verse if the literal meaning hinders the achievement of these goals.

It is important to note the cultural context in which the above verse was revealed in order to have a better understanding of how it was intended and how it can be used for the benefit of the family. In pre-Islamic Arabia, women were considered the property of men. If a man died, for example, his brother or his adult son could "inherit" the wife and take her for himself without her consent. If a man found his wife guilty of having an affair, killing her was a socially acceptable punishment.[29] In that cultural context, this verse served to protect women by introducing less destructive ways to address the problem. If a woman did not respond to verbal discussions, her husband could respond to the gravity of the situation by not sleeping with her, giving her the chance to realize the risks involved if she did not resume her commitment to the marriage. Finally, he could use something very light, like a tissue, to hit her. This process was very different, and much more constructive, than the standard response of that time.

Dr. Al-alwani suggests that in modern societies today, the third step in the process ("beating" the wife), is not to be applied because the circumstances of today's society are different from the society in which the Qur'an was revealed. He bases his opinion on the legislative rulings of the companions of the Prophet Muhammad and other jurists in this matter as well as other areas of Islamic law where rulings take into consideration the specific circumstances and elements of any given

---

29. Personal communication with Imam Mohamed Magid, Director of ADAMS Center, Herndon, VA, October 27, 2003.

issue.[30] Emphasis is placed on the spirit of the verse, which is the protection of the family unit from a real threat to its survival. In today's world, beating one's wife would surely lead to the very destruction of the family unit that this verse seeks to preserve.

Looking at the life of the Prophet Muhammad (PBUH) as an example of how these serious problems could be addressed is very informative. He was known for never hitting a woman or a child and for being strongly against the use of any type of violence. In reference to men who use violence at home, the Prophet said, "Could any of you beat his wife as he would beat a slave, and then lie with her in the evening?"[31] He also said, "Never beat God's handmaidens (female believers)."[32] He was a man whom his wife described as having internalized the teachings of the Qur'an in his character and personality.

The Prophet himself was put in several situations where he could have beaten his wives had he chosen to apply the verses with the literal interpretation. His wives sometimes caused him a lot of trouble, conspiring against him out of jealousy for another wife. Once, his wife Aisha, was even accused of adultery by some members of the community.[33] In none of these situations did he ever raise a hand or even his voice. He gave his wives options when they complained, and allowed Aisha to stay at her father's house for a month at her request, until her innocence was established.

---

30. Personal Communication, Taha Jabir Al-alwani, President of the Graduate School of Islamic Social Sciences, Leesburg, Virginia.

31. Narrated in the *hadith* collections of Bukhari and Muslim.

32. Cited by Asad, p. 110.

33. Adultery is a serious offense in the Islamic context. A claim of adultery is grounds for a legal proceeding.

Other issues leading to conflict should be solved by communication and problem-solving techniques. If a couple cannot resolve these issues on their own, each spouse is advised to bring a trusted person to represent him/her for arbitration. Any available resource that might help in solving the problem should be explored. In addition to arbitration or mediation using family members, counseling and anger management classes should be pursued. In the event that all efforts fail to resolve the problem, divorce can be considered as an option.

DIVORCE: A PEACEFUL SOLUTION

Divorce is allowed in Islam as a last resort when all other efforts at resolving conflict have been used. It is permitted under a wide variety of circumstances, but is especially acceptable when there is any cruelty involved. Divorce in Islam may differ from its meaning and laws in the United States. It can be initiated by either party, but the procedure and process varies depending on who initiates the divorce, and the circumstances around the divorce. It should be noted that there are different schools of thought and that some leaders may be more conservative than others in the matter of divorce.

The Qur'an devotes an entire chapter to the details of divorce.[34] Emphasis is placed on ensuring spousal and children's rights, acknowledging that these rights are often abused. The Qur'an holds not only each spouse accountable for making sure these rights are not violated, but also warns the entire community of being punished if these rights are not upheld.[35] Although there may be hurt feelings on both sides, the Qur'an advises decision-making from a compassionate stance, encouraging the couple to remember anything good that they shared. If the husband initiates the divorce, there are certain conditions under which his pronouncement of divorce must be made. For example, a pronouncement of divorce during extreme anger or under the influence of an intoxicant may be considered invalid. After the divorce pronouncement is made, there is a three-month period during which the wife remains in her home. The

---

34. Chapter 65, entitled "Divorce."

35. *"How many populations that insolently opposed the command of their Lord and of His messengers did We not then call to severe account? And We imposed on them an exemplary punishment?"* (65:8)

couple should continue normal interactions, except for having any sexual relations. This period is provided to allow for any opportunities of reconciliation. If this time period comes to an end without any desire for reconciliation, then the divorce is completed. The husband cannot take back any gifts he has given his wife, and remains responsible for spousal and child support.

The wife can also initiate divorce whether she has just cause or not. If she initiates divorce in the absence of any cruelty or mistreatment, she forfeits her right to keep any gifts, including her dowry. The wife of one of the companions of the Prophet asked the Prophet for a divorce saying that she couldn't stand to live with him despite having no criticism of his character or his religiosity. The Prophet asked her to return the garden he had given her and ordered her husband to accept the garden and release her from marriage.[36]

In the event that a woman is being abused or mistreated, there are several steps she can take. First, she should try advising her husband or having someone else advise him. Efforts should be made to seek counseling or anger management in order to improve the situation. If all efforts fail, then she has the option of ending the marriage. The Qur'an says, *"If a wife fears cruelty or desertion on her husband's part there is no blame on them if they arrange an amicable settlement between themselves; and such settlement is best...but if they disagree (and must part), God will provide abundance for all from His All-Reaching bounty: For God is He that cares for all and is wise."* (2:128,130). Finally, the community should be advised of the actions of an abuser in order to prevent him from abusing again in future relationships. The Prophet (PBUH) advised one woman, Asma, not to marry a particular man

---

36. Cited in Bukhari, *Book of Divorce*, # 4867.

because he was known to beat women.[37]

The psychological state of those impacted by divorce is also addressed in the Qur'an. The theme of forgiveness is tied to being conscious of God and is linked to the healing process. Strategies leading to forgiveness include focusing on the positive aspects that existed in the relationship in order to prevent hatred and anger from taking over, controlling one's anger to avoid acting unjustly, and increasing one's prayers. Furthermore, the awareness that God is aware of everything that happens and that He will ensure justice ultimately facilitates the process of forgiveness and may reduce any impulses to seek revenge.

Despite the permissibility of divorce, in many cultures that are predominantly Muslim, such as the Middle Eastern culture, divorced women may be stigmatized even if they have been mistreated by their husbands. These women may also experience difficulty obtaining a divorce from the court. Some countries' laws deny women their rights as Muslims; these countries are not applying Islamic law because they often contradict Qur'anic teachings. Women from these countries may struggle a great deal when trying to decide whether to leave an abusive home or remain there. In these situations, it is important to understand the cultural impact on the victim's decision-making process while reminding her of the religious permissibility of ending the marriage. Women from these countries may struggle with tremendous feelings of guilt and shame. Connecting these women to a religious community that is supportive can greatly facilitate her experience. Consulting with a religious leader in the community can also help both workers and victims to better understand the Islamic guidelines regarding divorce.

---

37. Personal communication with Mohammad Magid, Director of ADAMS Center. *Hadith* cited in Abu Shaqqah, Abdul Halim, *Tahrir al-Mar'ah fi `Asr al-Risalah*, 1990, V. 5.

Child Custody

The Qur'an does not specify which parent should have custody of the children in case of a divorce. However, the traditions of the Prophet Muhammad (PBUH) provide guidance in this matter. There are several instances of parents asking the Prophet (PBUH) to help resolve custody disputes. On one occasion he said, "The one who separates a mother from her child, God will separate between him and his beloved one on the Day of Judgment." In other instances, he allowed the child to choose which parent to live with.[38]

There are significant differences of opinion among the various Muslim schools of thought regarding child custody. In general, child custody is divided into two stages. The first stage applies to very young children; most scholars agree that at this stage, children should remain with their mother. During the second stage, most schools of thought recommend that boys live with their fathers after the age of 7 to 9; while girls should remain with their mothers. The rationale here is that children benefit from living with the parent of the same gender in order to have a role model and to be socialized properly. The differences in rulings between the major schools of thought reflect the positioning of that school as to whether the focus in determining custody is primarily on the welfare of the child versus on the welfare of the mother. Regardless, parents are advised not to allow their differences to impact the child. They should avoid involving the children in their own conflict and from using the children to get back at the other parent.

---

38. Cited in Roald, Anne Sofie. *Women in Islam: the Western Experience*. 2001. pp. 230-232.

Tools For The Worker

Most people trained to work in the area of domestic violence are familiar with the power and control wheel.[39] It is often used to help victims and perpetrators understand the dynamics of domestic violence. What follows will be an Islamic perspective on the spokes of the wheel. Workers will find this perspective useful in facilitating acceptance and understanding of how the types of abuse mentioned in the wheel are completely unacceptable in Islam, and therefore to God. Many Muslim women struggle because of their culturally ingrained belief that their husbands have the right to treat them in ways that are abusive by virtue of his position as head of the family. Hence, these women also are reluctant to take any action to stop the abusive behavior because of their belief or fear that God will be angry with them for disobeying their husbands or for taking any action that may lead to the destruction of the family unit. Of course, abusers play on these fears and beliefs as a form of psychological abuse in order to maintain the status quo.

Power and Control Wheel: Islamic Perspective

(Intimidation) Given the principle of tranquility that is a necessary criterion of an Islamic marriage, behaviors that instill fear in the other spouse are unacceptable. Even in the case where a relationship has deteriorated to the point of divorce, the Qur'an prohibits taking advantage of the spouse in any way. *"When you divorce women, and they*

---

39. See Appendix 2 for replication of Power and Control Wheel.

are about to fulfill the term of their `iddah [40], *either retain them back or let them go, but do not retain them to injure them (or) take undue advantage; if any one does that, he wrongs his own soul...."* (2:231). Instead, the Qur'an instructs the spouses to remember any positive aspects or experiences that were shared, and to respect the relationship that was shared by being respectful and just to each other. *"...the husbands should either retain their wives together on equitable terms or let them go with kindness..."* (2:229).

(**Emotional Abuse**) Muslims are enjoined by the Qur'an and the teachings of their Prophet to be very careful about offending or insulting others. Believers are prohibited from calling other people names, mocking others, or putting them down in any way. *"O you who believe! Let not some people among you laugh at others. It may be that the (latter) are better than the former: nor defame nor be sarcastic to each other, nor call each other by offensive nicknames: ill-seeming is a name connoting wickedness, (to be used by one) after he has believed: and those who do not desist are (indeed) doing wrong."* (49:11). In addition, the Qur'an warns that being suspicious of each other leads to the sins of spying and backbiting, and should thus be avoided. *"O you who believe! Avoid suspicion as much as possible. For suspicion in some cases is a sin. And spy not on each other, nor speak ill of each other behind their backs...."* (49:12). The Prophet (PBUH) said, "Muslims are brothers (and sisters). They should not betray or humiliate each other."[41]

---

40. `*Iddah* refers to the three-month separation period between husband and wife that must occur prior to the completion of a divorce. During this period, the couple continues to reside in the same home and maintain civil relations. If there are no sexual relations during this time, the divorce is complete at the end of the duration. The purpose of the *iddah* is to allow for any opportunity for reconciliation that might occur as they reflect on the possibility of impending divorce.

41. Cited in the collection of Tirmidhi, Book 27, No. 1850.

(**Isolation**) Islam emphasizes social and family relations and recognizes connections to others as a basic human need. Every Muslim has a responsibility to maintain good relations with relatives, neighbors, and others in the community. The Qur'an associates treating others well with worshiping God: *"Serve God, and join not any partners with Him; and do good---to parents, kinsfolk, orphans, those in need, neighbors who are near, neighbors who are strangers, the companion by your side, the wayfarer (you meet)..."* (4:36).

No one has the right to deny another person the opportunity for social interaction. In fact, most teachings in Islam apply to relational contexts and govern interactions between people. Many forms of worship are communal or congregational. For example, Muslims are encouraged to participate in social functions, to celebrate with others, to visit the sick, and to provide support for one another in times of hardship. The Prophet (PBUH) declined a dinner invitation repeatedly until his wife was also invited, refusing to leave her behind.[42]

(**Using Blame**) Every person is individually responsible for his/her own actions and cannot blame another person for his/her mistakes. The Qur'an says, *"If anyone earns a fault or a sin and throws it on to one that is innocent, he carries (on himself) (both) a falsehood and a flagrant sin."* (4:112). On the Day of Judgment, each person will be held accountable separate from his/her spouse, parent, child, etc. The Qur'an says, *"Namely, that no bearer of burdens can bear the burden of another; that a person can have nothing but what one strives for; that the fruit of one's striving will soon come in sight, then will one be rewarded with a reward*

---

42. Cited in Abu Shaqqah, *Tahrir al Mar'ah*, Vol. 1, p. 306.

complete." (53:38-41).[43] False accusations, particularly in the case of a woman's chastity, have severe punishment. *"And those who launch a charge against chaste women, and produce not four witnesses (to support their allegations) flog them with eighty stripes, and reject their evidence ever after, for such men are wicked transgressors."* (24:4).

(**Using Children**) Islam protects and guarantees the rights of children. They should not be subject to any harsh treatment nor witness any abuse. Muslim jurists make their rulings in family matters by considering the child's benefit before the adult's. The Prophet Muhammad (PBUH) was known to interact with children in the most gentle and respectful manner possible. During times of conflict, the Qur'an reminds spouses that ...*"no mother shall be treated unfairly on account of her child. Nor father on account of his child..."* (2:233).

(**Using sexual abuse**) Human sexuality is fully recognized in Islam and is considered normal, healthy and righteous when expressed in the proper marital context.[44] In restricting sexual relations to married partners, Islam views marital sex as an act of obedience to God in which the values of Islam must be observed. Each partner's needs must be taken into consideration, and each one has the right to a fulfilling relationship. Even in this intimate relationship, God's presence is a reminder for considerate and compassionate treatment of one's spouse. However, the sexual relationship is to be guarded with strict confidentiality and details are not to be discussed with others (except for the purpose of treatment).

---

43. Also, *"Whoever receives guidance, receives it for his/her own benefit; whoever goes astray does so to his/her own loss. No bearer of burdens can bear the burden of another, nor would We make Our wrath visit until We had sent a messenger (to give warning."* (17:15)

44. Personal communication, Imam Johari Abdul Malik, Muslim Chaplin, Howard University

In addition to restricting the sexual relationship to marriage, the Qur'an also established boundaries on whom one can marry (or have a sexual relationship with).[45] Ones parents, siblings, children, aunts, uncles, nieces, nephews, and spouse's parents are all people to whom one cannot be married. These boundaries are protective and serve to prevent abuse and incest.

Sexual abuse can occur when force is used by either party, especially to have sex in a manner or time that is prohibited. For example, Islam prohibits anal sex, intercourse during the wife's menstrual cycle[46], and any sexual relations while fasting.[47] When one spouse intentionally or consistently minimizes, invalidates or ignores the sexual needs or desires of the other spouse, abuse is also occurring.

Workers should be aware that issues related to sexuality may be very difficult for victims to discuss. In many cultures, this is a taboo subject. Furthermore, societal views on the sexual rights and responsibilities of husbands and wives may make disclosure more complicated. For example, in many Eastern countries it is culturally accepted that husbands have unlimited sexual rights to their wives, regardless of how she may feel. Therefore, the conceptualization of marital rape rarely exists in the

---

45. See Qur'an 4:23.

46. *"They ask you concerning women's courses. Say, They are a hurt and a pollution. So keep away from women in their courses, and do not approach them until they are clean. But when they have purified themselves, you may approach them in any manner, time or place ordained for you by God. For God loves those who turn to Him constantly and He loves those who keep themselves pure and clean."* (2:222). What is meant here by staying away from women during menstruation is strictly abstinence from intercourse; otherwise, all interaction is normal, including the display of affection.

47. *"Permitted to you on the night of the fast is the approach to your wives. They are your garments and you are their garments..."* (2:187)

Muslim world, although it may not be uncommon for women to be forced (either physically, or psychologically by using guilt) to have sexual relations within the marital relationship. This type of abuse may not be reported initially, but is should be gently inquired about.

Regarding children who have been sexually abused by a family member, workers should anticipate that the family and the community may put a great deal of pressure on the child to prevent him or her from reporting, or later to get the child to recant. This pressure is a result of a combination of factors: denial that this type of abuse occurs, unwillingness to believe that a family member could be capable of such an atrocity, shame, mistaken belief that a female child must have provoked it, and wanting to protect the reputation of the family. In the case of girls who have been sexually violated, there is also the fear that if her experience becomes known to others, her chances of getting married will suffer due to the high cultural value placed on virginity.

(**Using economic abuse**) It is the responsibility of Muslim men to provide for women financially. The Qur'an say, *"Men are the protectors and maintainers of women, because God has given the one more than the other, and because of the sustenance they provide from their own means..."*(4:34). Men should not make women feel humiliated or in debted to them because it is a Muslim woman's right to be taken care of financially. Even if he is unable to provide for her fully, she has the choice of working outside the home but is not required to contribute to household expenses. In the event that a husband has the means to support his family but withholds money, the wife has the right to take what she needs for herself and the children (within reason) without his permission.

In the case of marital dispute or threat of divorce, a husband should not threaten financial hardship as a means to prevent his wife from leaving. *"O you who believe! You are forbidden to inherit women against their will. Nor should you treat them with harshness, that you may take away part of the dowry you have given them—except where they have been guilty of open lewdness. On the contrary, live with them on a footing of kindness and equality. If you take a dislike to them, it may be that you dislike a good thing, and God brings about through it a great deal of good. But if you decide to take one wife in place of another, even if you had given the latter a whole treasure of dowry, take not the least bit of it back. Would you take it by slander and a manifest wrong? And how could you take it when you have gone in unto each other, and they have taken from you a solemn covenant?"* (4:19-21).

The Concept of Accountability

The significance of accountability in the area of domestic violence is related to the batterer's acknowledgment to himself, the victim, and all battered women that he has committed abuses that are unacceptable in society. The Islamic concept of accountability is much broader and much more absolute. There are two levels of accountability in Islam: primary accountability is to God, and secondary accountability is to oneself and other human beings. Muslims believe that God is watching all people at all times, recording all individuals' actions in order to hold them accountable on the Day of Judgment. God's laws that govern human behavior are absolute, as compared to laws designed by human governments or societies. In Islam, there is no dichotomy; rather, in order to be considered Islamic, all laws should be consistent with divine instruction. Because of this, crimes against people are also considered as sins, and can be judged in this world (through courts and legal mechanisms) as well as the hereafter.

Repentance

Repentance in Islam is a simple process that occurs on multiple levels. The first step is at the intrapersonal level: the batterer must face him/herself and admit that there is a problem. This step is addressed in the Qur'an, *"And those who, having done something to be ashamed of, or wronged their own souls, earnestly bring God to mind, and ask for forgiveness for their sins—and who can forgive sins except God?—and are never obstinate in persisting knowingly in (the wrong) they have done."* (3:135). The second step is to show regret of the action and to repent immediately. The Qur'an says, *"God accepts the repentance of those who do evil in ignorance and repent soon afterwards; to them will God turn in mercy; for God is full of knowledge and wisdom"* (3:17). Finally, the third level of repentance is accepting full responsibility for the evil deeds committed. This level involves two steps: immediately discontinuing the abuse and establishing a new lifestyle that is not conducive to further abuse. God says in the Qur'an, *"Those who repent and make amends and openly declare (the truth); to them I turn, for I am oft-returning, most merciful"* (2:160) Also, the Prophet Muhammad (PBUH) said, "If anyone of you hurt someone in any way, go quickly and ask forgiveness before the time passes and you pay off in the hereafter."[48] The Qur'an encourages people to *"establish regular prayers at the end of the day and at the approaches of the night. For those things that are good remove those that are evil..."* (11:114).

---

48. Narrated by Al-Bukhari..

Useful Interventions with Muslims

Interventions with Muslims should maintain a family focus. Having a family focus affects the way interventions are designed and implemented, as well as the overall goals of the worker and the victim. While the safety of the victim is always the first priority, it must be remembered that the family, not the individual, is the basic unit of the Muslim society. All interventions and treatment plans should consider the benefit of the family as a unit, in addition to the safety of the individual members. Ideally, interventions should achieve safety for the victims, treatment for the offenders, and preservation of the family unit whenever possible. Of course, separation of the victim from the abuser may be necessary initially, and divorce may be an eventual consequence. However, divorce should be held as a final option when all others have been exhausted.

While Muslim victims may be American citizens, they may also be immigrants, refugees or asylees. The background and legal status of the victim are significant variables in planning interventions and in the resulting outcomes. Culture and religion may interact in many ways, leading to a wide range of responses in Muslim victims. It is important to assess the impact of underlying cultural values when intervening with a family experiencing domestic violence. On the other hand, one must not be too quick to explain all issues as cultural ones; there are often underlying emotional or mental health issues, in addition to idiosyncrasies in a particular family or individual. The following tips may be helpful in beginning to develop effective interventions.

TIPS

Assess

• **Degree of acculturation**: More acculturated women will be more familiar with the concepts of domestic violence, the resources available, the legal system, etc. They may also be better prepared to be self-sufficient due to education or work experience.

• **English comprehension**: It is important to ascertain the need for an interpreter. Among non-English speakers, comprehension levels are usually better than the ability to express themselves. However, many times misunderstandings occur between the worker and the victim due to misinterpreting key words despite good overall comprehension of English. Avoid relying on the victim's children to interpret. Try to use professionals to interpret whenever possible.

• **Underlying trauma**: Many immigrant Muslims have come from war-torn countries and have experienced trauma either from witnessing events related to war or in the process of fleeing the country. Underlying trauma can affect both the victim and the perpetrator and should be identified and treated because it can exacerbate violence in the home, as well as compound the trauma of the domestic violence.

Identify

• **Reasons for immigration**: Knowing the history can provide important clues to understanding the domestic violence and planning appropriate treatment. Sometimes, the abuse begins after the family comes to the United States and can indicate depression or other mental illnesses that need to be treated.

- **Stressors**: These can include role-reversal, change in socio-economic status due to necessary career changes, financial hardship, culture shock, loss of extended family, language barriers, inability to access appropriate resources, etc.

- **Relevant religious and cultural issues**: In addition to understanding the religious and cultural beliefs about domestic violence, workers should inquire about any particular needs a victim may have if she chooses to go to a shelter. Some of these needs may include identifying a space which the victim can use for prayer, making sure food does not contain any pork or alcohol products, and providing appropriate clothing. Asking the victim about special needs she may have in order to accommodate her religious practices will be greatly appreciated and will increase the victim's comfort level.

Expect

- **Polite nodding or verbal agreement with possible non-compliance**: In many Eastern cultures, assertiveness is not valued. It is impolite and disrespectful to disagree with an authority figure. Therefore, it is not unusual that in the beginning of the relationship with the worker, victims may seem to be in agreement while not following through later with recommendations.

- **More time needed to build rapport and trust**: The roles of victim advocate, therapist, shelter worker, etc may be unfamiliar to immigrant women. Suspicion and distrust may be a result of Muslim women's fear that Western workers are biased toward divorce, guilt about seeking help outside the family or community, and uncertainty about the choices she will be asked to make.

Explain

- **"The system"**: Take time to explain clearly the role and limitation of the advocate, the shelter, the court, and the laws. Explanations may need to be repeated without the use of jargon and taking care to use simple, clear language with limited-English speakers.

- **The law**: While most women know that they can call 911 if they are being hurt, they often do not know what will happen once the authorities arrive. They may be surprised when the abuser is arrested, or dismayed to find out they cannot stop the prosecution by dropping the charges.

- **The cycle of violence**: Many Muslim women confuse the concept of forgiveness with tolerance for the abuse. Emphasize the probability that the abuse will escalate or become more severe without intervention.

- **Impact on the children**: Many women believe it is more important for children to live with both parents than for children to live in a safe, non-violent home. Explaining the long-term psychological effects on the children of living in a violent home can often help women make the choices they need to secure safety for themselves and their children.

- **Consequences for the abuser**: Women need to understand what events will be set in motion once they make a police report. These consequences can be framed as part of the process of accountability that abusers must experience in order to change and create the possibility for a future healthy relationship.

Share

- **Success stories**: Knowing how other Muslim women have survived, ended the violence, coped with the potential negative response of other Muslims, and created healthier environments for their children can be inspirational and motivational to victims.

• **Some personal information**: Sharing general information about yourself to the extent that you are comfortable, will help to establish rapport and trust. Sharing information about your children, your faith, or your experience with other Muslims will decrease suspicion and anxiety while facilitating the development of a relationship with the victim.

Gender Issues

• **Use same gender provider**: Whenever possible, victims should be allowed to work with workers of the same gender, especially when dealing with matters of sexuality. Practicing Muslims do not interact as casually with the opposite gender as is common in American society. Furthermore, issues related to sexuality are taboo and will be easier to discuss with providers of the same gender.

• **Eye contact**: Between genders, eye contact may be uncomfortable, especially for less acculturated women. Interpret avoided eye contact as a sign of respect.

• **Shaking hands**: Always ask before shaking hands with Muslims of the opposite gender. Some Muslims refrain from this practice out of modesty.

Utilize Strengths

• **Faith/spirituality**: Both victims and abusers can use their faith and religious beliefs to facilitate change. Victims may use their faith for strength, encouragement, and patience. Knowing that God is always with them can be a great comfort during a time when others may not be supportive.

- **Islam teaches personal accountability**: This concept is important for the abuser to be willing to learn new ways of interacting, as well as for the victim to take responsibility for her own safety and well-being.

- **Concept of forgiveness**: Islam teaches that all people are susceptible to making mistakes. God promises forgiveness of all sins, with the exception of worshipping other gods, if one genuinely repents. Islam encourages people to forgive each other and to give second chances, provided there is evidence that the guilty party is making efforts to change his/her behavior.

- **Importance of the children**: Many women are more likely to make changes for the sake of their children than for themselves. Focusing on the well-being of the children is often a significant motivator for women to seek and maintain safety.

- **Protection of the family**: Victims may respond better to a focus on the preservation, as much as possible, of the family unit than to a focus on the victim ending the marriage. Frame interventions as being protective of all the individuals in the family. Even the abuser is unsafe in a violent home.

BUILDING BRIDGES

- **Community leaders**: Build relationships with leaders in the Muslim community who can be a source of support to the worker, the victim, and the abuser. Many times, when the victim knows that an imam is in agreement with the interventions being used, the worker is given more credibility. Trust is gained more easily, making the work less challenging. Community leaders can also identify other resources within the community, such as social service programs and support groups.

• **Community workers**: As Muslim communities are increasing their awareness about the existence and nature of domestic violence among their families, there are more individuals within the community acting as advocates. Connecting with these workers can be an invaluable source of support since they are familiar with the community's internal resources.

• **Educational workshops**: Build awareness by having educational meetings in community centers and mosques. Many people will feel more comfortable learning about domestic violence in these non-threatening and familiar settings. This type of outreach leads to relationships within the community, increased trust and willingness to work collaboratively.

• **Increase awareness of services**: Invite Muslim community leaders and members to agencies and worksites to familiarize them with the services that are provided and how to access them. Describe what women's shelters are like to dispel myths and anxieties that may exist.

Appendix 1:
Compilation of Qur'anic Verses Cited in this Paper

"Let there be no compulsion in religion. Truth stands out clear from Error. Whoever rejects Evil and believes in God has grasped the most trustworthy Handhold, that never breaks" (2:256).

Say, the truth is from your Lord. Let him who will, believe, and let him who will, reject (it): For the wrongdoers We have prepared a fire whose smoke and flames, like the walls and roof of a tent, will hem them in....As to those who believe and work righteousness...for them will be gardens of Eternity, beneath them rivers will flow..." (18:29-31).

"Therefore do give admonition, for you are one to admonish. You are not one to manage (people's) affairs. But if any turns away and rejects God, God will punish him with a mighty punishment." (88:21-24).

"God commands justice, the doing of good, and liberality to kith and kin, and He forbids all shameful deeds, and injustice and rebellion. He instructs you, that you may receive admonition" (16:90).

"O you who believe! Stand out firmly for God as witnesses to fair dealing, and let not the hatred of others to you make you swerve to wrong and depart you from justice. Be just: that is next to piety. And fear God. For God is well-acquainted with all that you do" (5:8).

"O mankind! Reverence your guardian-Lord, who created you from a single soul. Created, of like nature, its mate, and from them twain scattered (like seeds) countless men and women—fear God, through Whom you demand your mutual (rights), and (reverence) the wombs (that bore you), for God ever watches over you" (4:1).

"O mankind! We created you from a single (pair) of a male and a female, and made you into nations and tribes, that you may know each other (not that you may despise each other). Verily, the most honored of you in the sight of God is the most righteous of you..." (49:13).

"The blame is only against those who oppress people with wrongdoing and insolently transgress beyond bounds through the land, defying right and justice. For such (people) there will be a grievous penalty. But indeed if any show patience and forgive, that would truly be an exercise of courageous will and resolution in the conduct of affairs" (42:42-43).

"And those who, when an oppressive wrong is inflicted on them, (are not cowed) but help and defend themselves. The recompense for an injury is an injury equal thereto (in degree), but if a person forgives and makes reconciliation, his reward is due from God, for (God) loves not those who do wrong" (42: 39-40).

"We ordained therein for them: life for life, eye for eye, nose for nose, ear for ear, tooth for tooth, and wounds equal for equal. But if anyone remits the retaliation by way of charity, it is an act

of atonement for himself. And if any fail to judge by (the light of) what God has revealed, they are (no better than) wrongdoers." (5:45).

"When angels take the souls of those who die in sin against their souls, they say, "In what (plight) were you?" They reply, "Weak and oppressed were we in the earth." They say, "Was not the earth of God spacious enough for you to move yourselves away (from evil)?" Such [people] will find their abode in hell—what an evil refuge! Except those who are (really) weak and oppressed—men, women, and children who have no means in their power, nor (a guidepost) to direct their way. For those there is hope that God will forgive. For God does blot out (sins) and is oft-forgiving" (4:98-99).

"And among His signs is this: that He created for you mates from among yourselves, that you may dwell in tranquility with them, and He has put love and mercy between your (hearts). Verily in that are signs for those who reflect" (30:21).

"And in nowise covet those things in which God has bestowed His gifts more freely on some of you than on others: to men is allotted what they earn, and to women what they earn. But ask God of His bounty. For God has full knowledge of all things." (4:32).

"...those who avoid the greater crimes and shameful deeds, and, when they are angry even then forgive; those who hearken to their Lord, and establish regular prayer; who (conduct) their affairs by mutual consultation..." (2:37-38).

"Let the women live in the same style as you live, according to your means: Do not annoy them, so as to restrict them, and if they carry (life in their wombs) spend your substance on them until they deliver their burden, and if they suckle your children give them their recompense: and take mutual counsel together according to what is just and reasonable, and if you find yourselves in difficulties, let another woman suckle the child on the father's behalf." (65:6).

"The mothers shall give suck to their offspring for two whole years, if the father desires to complete the term. But he shall bear the cost of their food and clothing on equitable terms. No soul shall have a burden laid on it greater than it can bear. No mother shall be treated unfairly on account of her child. Nor father on account of his child, an heir shall be chargeable in the same way. If they both decide on weaning by mutual consent, and after due consultation, there is no blame on them. If you decide on a wet-nurse for your offspring there is no blame on you provided you pay (the mother) what you offered, on equitable terms. But fear God and know that God sees well what you do." (2:233).

"0 my son! Join not in worship (others) with God: for false worship is indeed the highest wrongdoing...If there be (but) the weight of a mustard seed and it were (hidden) in a rock, or anywhere in the heavens or on the earth, God will bring it forth: For God understands the finer mysteries and is well- acquainted

(with them). O my son! Establish regular prayer, enjoin what is just, and forbid what is wrong, and bear with patient constancy whatever betide thee; for this is firmness (of purpose) in the conduct of affairs. And swell not thy cheek with pride at men, nor walk in insolence through the earth; for God loves not any arrogant boaster. And be moderate in pace, and lower thy voice; for the harshest of sounds without doubt is the braying of the ass." (31:12-19).

"Invite to the way of your Lord with wisdom and beautiful preaching; and argue with them in ways that are best and most gracious." (16:125).

"It is part of the mercy of God that thou dost deal gently with them. Wert thou severe or harsh-hearted, they would have broken away from about thee: so pass over (their faults), and ask for (God's) forgiveness for them; and consult them in affairs (of moment) (3:159).

"Men shall take full care of women with the bounties which God has bestowed more abundantly on the former than on the latter, and with what they may spend out of their possessions. And the righteous women are the truly devout ones, who guard the intimacy which God has [ordained to be guarded]. And as for those women whose ill-will you have reason to fear, admonish them [first]; then leave them alone in bed; then beat them; and if thereupon they pay you heed, do not seek to harm them. Behold, God is indeed most high, great! And if you have reason to fear that a breach might occur between a [married] couple, appoint

an arbiter from among his people and an arbiter from among her people; if they both want to set things aright, God may bring about their reconciliation. Behold, God is indeed all-knowing, aware." (4:34-35).

"If a wife fears cruelty or desertion on her husband's part there is no blame on them if they arrange an amicable settlement between themselves; and such settlement is best...but if they disagree (and must part), God will provide abundance for all from His All-Reaching bounty: For God is He that cares for all and is wise." (2:128,130).

"When you divorce women, and they are about to fulfill the term of their `iddah, either retain them back or let them go, but do not retain them to injure them (or) take undue advantage; if any one does that, he wrongs his own soul...." (2:231).

"O you who believe! Let not some people among you laugh at others. It may be that the (latter) are better than the former: nor defame nor be sarcastic to each other, nor call each other by offensive nicknames: ill-seeming is a name connoting wickedness, (to be used by one) after he has believed: and those who do not desist are (indeed) doing wrong." (49:11).

"O you who believe! Avoid suspicion as much as possible. For suspicion in some cases is a sin. And spy not on each other, nor speak ill of each other behind their backs...." (49:12).

"Serve God, and join not any partners with Him; and do good--to parents, kinsfolk, orphans, those in need, neighbors who are near, neighbors who are strangers, the companion by your side, the wayfarer (you meet)..." (4:36).

"If anyone earns a fault or a sin and throws it on to one that is innocent, he carries (on himself) (both) a falsehood and a flagrant sin." (4:112).

"Namely, that no bearer of burdens can bear the burden of another; that a person can have nothing but what one strives for; that the fruit of one's striving will soon come in sight, then will one be rewarded with a reward complete." (53:38-41).

"And those who launch a charge against chaste women, and produce not four witnesses (to support their allegations) flog them with eighty stripes, and reject their evidence ever after, for such men are wicked transgressors." (24:4).

"They ask you concerning women's courses. Say, They are a hurt and a pollution. So keep away from [having sex with] women in their courses, and do not approach them until they are clean. But when they have purified themselves, you may approach them in any manner, time or place ordained for you by God. For God loves those who turn to Him constantly and He loves those who keep themselves pure and clean." (2:222).

"Permitted to you on the night of the fasts is the approach to your wives. They are your garments and you are their garments..." (2:187).

"O you who believe! You are forbidden to inherit women against their will. Nor should you treat them with harshness, that you may take away part of the dowry you have given them—except where they have been guilty of open lewdness. On the contrary, live with them on a footing of kindness and equality. If you take a dislike to them, it may be that you dislike a good thing, and God brings about through it a great deal of good. But if you decide to take one wife in place of another, even if you had given the latter a whole treasure of dowry, take not the least bit of it back. Would you take it by slander and a manifest wrong? And how could you take it when you have gone in unto each other, and they have taken from you a solemn covenant?" (4:19-21).

"And those who, having done something to be ashamed of, or wronged their own souls, earnestly bring God to mind, and ask for forgiveness for their sins—and who can forgive sins except God?—and are never obstinate in persisting knowingly in (the wrong) they have done." (3:135).

"God accepts the repentance of those who do evil in ignorance and repent soon afterwards; to them will God turn in mercy; for God is full of knowledge and wisdom" (3:17).

"Those who repent and make amends and openly declare (the truth); to them I turn, for I am oft-returning, most merciful" (2:160).

"...establish regular prayers at the end of the day and at the approaches of the night. For those things that are good remove those that are evil..." (11:114).

Appendix 2:
Power & Control Wheel

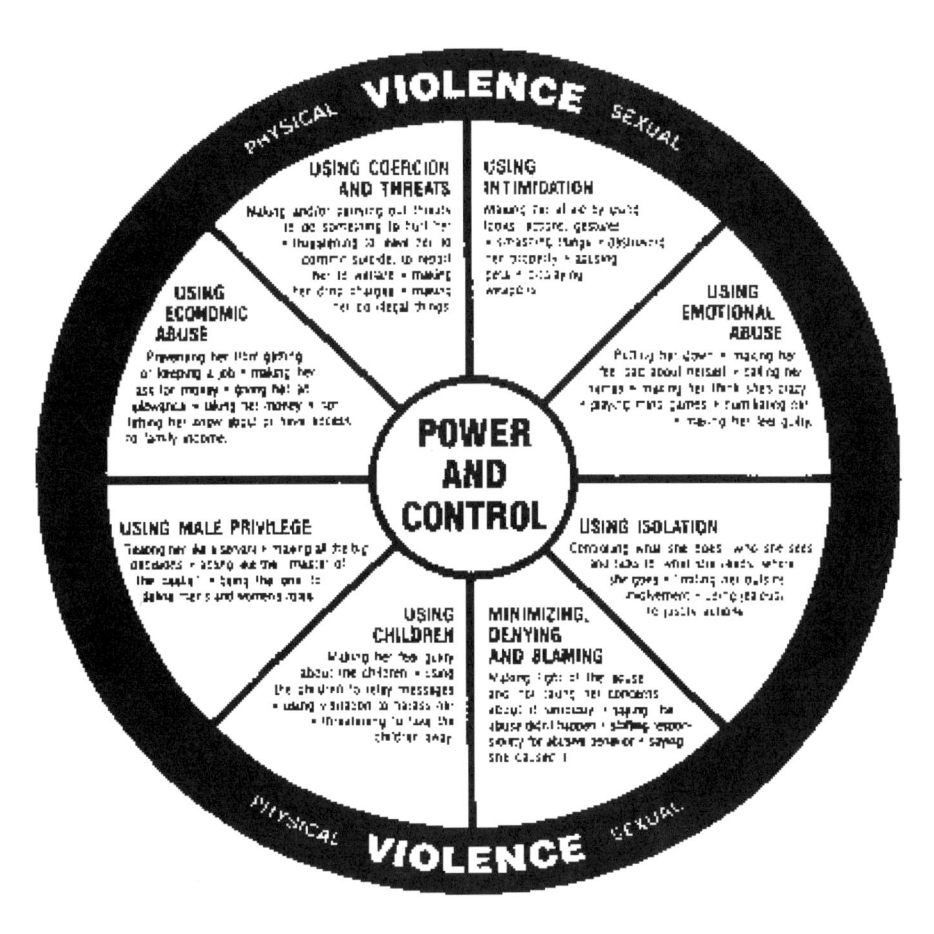

Domestic Abuse Intervention Project
202 East Superior Street
Duluth, Minnesota 55802
218-722-2781
www.duluth-model.org

Appendix 3:
ADDITIONAL READINGS AND USEFUL WEBSITES

ADDITIONAL READINGS:

Abdelkader, Deina. (2000). *Social Justice in Islam*. IIIT.

`Ali, Abdullah Yusuf. (1999). *The Meaning of the Holy Qur'an*. 10th Edition. Brentville, MD: Amana Publications.

al Faruqui, I. R. (1984). *Islam*. Brentwood, MD: International Graphics.

Asad, Muhammad. (1980). *The Message of the Qur'an*. Gibraltar: Dar al-Andalus.

Badawi, Jamal. (1982). *The Muslim Women's Dress According to Qur'an and Sunnah*. Taha Publishers.

Esposito, John. (2002). *What Everyone Needs to Know About Islam*.Oxford University Press.

Maqsud, Ruqaiyyah Waris. (2000). *Muslim Marriage Guide*. Brentwood, Maryland: Amana Publications.

Nanji, A.A. (1993). The Muslim family in North American: continuity and change. In H. P. McAdoo (Ed.), *Family Ethnicity: Strength in Diversity*. Newbury Park, CA: SAGE Publication, Inc.

Roald, Anne Sofie.(2001). *Women in Islam: the Western Experience.* NY: Routledge.

Syed, Ashfaque Ullah. (1998). *Index of Qur'anic Topics.* Washington, DC: IFTA Office.

Wadud, Amina. (1999). *Qur'an and Women.* Oxford University Press.

USEFUL WEBSITES:

American Arab Anti-Discrimination Committee Website:

http://www/adc.org/education/culture.htm

Council on American Islamic Relations:

www.cair-net.org

Islam Online:

www.islamonline.org

Islamic City:

www.islamiCity.org

SPONSORING ORGANIZATIONS

FOUNDATION FOR APPROPRIATE AND IMMEDIATE TEMPORARY HELP (FAITH)

Mission

The mission of the Foundation for Appropriate and Immediate Temporary Help (FAITH) is to work towards dignified and harmonious life and the development of safe and peaceful lives for the women and children. To provide humanitarian aid to those in need who live in the Northern Virginia communities. FAITH intends to establish a multi-purpose social service complex.

Some of the services FAITH provides
– Safe and Peaceful Families (Domestic Violence prevention program)
– Cultural sensitivity trainings in the area of domestic violence
– Community outreach seminars on education and prevention of domestic violence.
– Connecting the victim to county and private resources
– Court Advocacy
– Transportation to shelter
– Helping Hands (Financial Assistance)
– Car, computer and furniture donation
– Distribution of canned and dry food
– Job skills training
– Thrift store
– Burial expenses
– Congregational Health Ministry
– Research

FAITH is a member of
– Network against Family Abuse (NAFA)
– Domestic and Sexual violence coordinating council of Loudoun County
– Fairfax county community resource council.
– Fairfax county Faith Communities in Action (FCIA)
– Fairfax county FCIA Domestic Violence task force
– Mental Health and Substance Abuse Services (Fairfax County)

FAITH's sponsor and mentor organizations are
– Loudoun Abused Women Shelter (LAWS)
– Center for Multicultural Human Services (CMHS)

CENTER FOR MULTICULTURAL HUMAN SERVICES (CMHS)

Center for Multicultural Human Services (CMHS) is a licensed mental health and social services agency serving immigrants and refugees throughout the metropolitan Washington, DC area. Its mission is to help people from ethnically diverse backgrounds succeed by providing comprehensive, cultural sensitive mental health and related services and by conducting research and training to make such services more widely available.

INTERNATIONAL INSTITUTE OF ISLAMIC THOUGHT (IIIT)

The International Institute of Islamic Thought (IIIT) promotes academic research on the methodology and philosophy of various disciplines, and gives special emphasis to the development of Islamic scholarship in contemporary social sciences. The program, which has become known as "Islamization of Knowledge", endeavors to elucidate Islamic concepts that integrate Islamic revealed knowledge with human knowledge and revives Islamic ethical and moral knowledge.